Swimming into the Light

Swimming into the Light

by

Carolyn Marie Souaid

Cover art by Seymour Segal.
Cover design by Terry Gallagher/Doowah Design Inc.
Photograph of Carolyn Marie Souaid by Allen McInnis.

Acknowledgments
Many thanks to Michael Harris for his editorial assistance, Robert Allen for offering advice on the manuscript at various stages, and to my husband and family for their support and encouragement.

Grateful acknowledgement is made to the following publications, where some of these poems appeared in current or earlier draft forms—*Scrivener, The Antigonish Review, The Fiddlehead, Poetry Canada, The Urban Wanderers Reader* (Hochelaga Press).

Adrienne Rich, *Of Woman Born* (W.W. Norton Inc.)
Susan Glickman, "Mission Control" from *Hide & Seek* (Véhicule Press)

Published with the assistance of The Canada Council.
Printed and bound in Canada by Veilleux Impression.
Dépôt légal, the National Library of Canada and
la Bibliothèque nationale du Québec.

Canadian Cataloguing in Publication Data

Souaid, Carolyn Marie, 1959–
Swimming into the light

Poems.
ISBN 0-921833-43-1

I. Title.

PS8587.O87S94 1995 C811'.54 C95-900886-1
PR9199.3.S69S94 1995

NuAge Editions, P.O. Box 8, Station E
Montréal, Québec H2T 3A5

For my son, Alex

The “childless woman” and the “mother” are a false polarity…
Adrienne Rich

Our genes, ever sentimental, abhor singularity.
Susan Glickman

One

Infertility

There are shapes my body will never make—
the perfect O, for instance, that women form
to expel the gleaming apricot head of a newborn

part of their own flesh & their lover's
part of their mother & father & generations
before them, swimming into the light

the whole universe from beginning to end
falling through them
like the sweet green rain.

Telling My Mother

I tell her straight out
I can't have babies.

Me, eyeing minutiae—
small surge of her wrists
exposed goose bumps at the neck
her upturned palm, skin pulled taut across the bone

a vessel for the scattered shards.
Bent over, she scrapes her chair
along the kitchen floor, a chalky screech.

My mother, stoop-shouldered
bending from a dish of toast crumbs
groping the tile for glass
pale hair draining
into the floor.

Romper Room & JFK

My first memories
happened at three, drama of death
in the striated bone of his cheek
someone spooning ice cubes onto his tongue.
I kissed my grandfather goodbye
in the stuffy room, chorus of relatives
in bosomy black dresses.

After he died, Mom pestered the TV station
until they made me a guest on Romper Room
bought me a blue plastic purse
to match the ribbons in my hair. How I performed
for the camera, a regular Jackie Kennedy
until that shattering moment
when the clasp broke & my pennies ricocheted
off chairs & across the stage
sent me clamoring for the broken pieces
of my purse.

We drove to my grandfather's grave
flags half-mast, highway a blur.

Slow dark cars & then a rash of trees
like pall-bearers saluting the avenue.

Nothing fixed but the gestalt
of epic moments, like home movies
coded in the child, celluloid strands of DNA
speeding up, winding down
always just a hair
out of focus.

Photograph of My Grandfather

Somehow, in the middle of the Turkish War
he found time to pose for the camera
eyes staring squarely into the lens
bullets bandoliered across his lean chest.

He is a young man, kefaya draped
in elegant folds around his head, rifle locked
in his arm, feet slightly apart, waiting for the click
of the shutter.

Though he doesn't know it, he carries generations
in the sepia grain of his flesh, my mother, my aunts & uncles
my cousins, the lot of us his chromosome army
charging into infinity.

I knew him as a quiet man who boiled eggs for lunch
& wore long-johns to bed. The *Jiddo* who taught me checkers
in his noisy den off Spadina. I loved the smell of that room
the blue tins of Edgeworth tobacco. I loved the way
his long, hairless finger tapped the rosewood pipe

the way his sharp blue eye
never once left the game.

Rites

1.

The period before lunch
the nurse showed films of thin girls giggling
at the seashore, flow charts & arrows
navigating eggs through the heady waters
of their private parts.

She passed around a sanitary napkin, clean white wing
pleated in flight, crisp as a salt breeze—
were it not for soup wafting in from the cafeteria.

Heather threw up while I tossed in my seat
golden peach hair glistening between my legs

certain that none of this
would ever happen to me.

2.

How is it the class hunk always
picked a Barbie or Cathy, someone blonde & built
& flunking out of school—the rest of us left
to imagine the marriage of gin & Juicy Fruit
as they necked in some backseat
on a hot spring night.

Plain, pimpled girls, we walked home alone
soda-fantasies still reeling on the dance floor
nipples ripening our sensible blouses while the bulb of his cock
gave it to us through his stiff pair of jeans.

Ask anyone—
we aced every assignment, every class test
except the one in the humid gym, the young
green bodies of boys feeling their way
in the dark.

3.

In grade 9, the seasons changed me—
chest pushing up my tunic
baring legs & awkward knees
scarred by the playground.

I joined the Leona-crowd
wore a brown-pronged comb
in my hair & lipstick

joined &
smoked cigarettes &
kissed boys

thorny laughter
leaving a bloodless trail
of petals.

Bible Camp

We shivered in cold flannel, the last of our bonfire
faces blazing the pine-dark

crawled into sleeping bags, 13-year-old bodies touching
like two small embers on the sprawling earth floor.
All night, I watched him sleep

kindling my future
in the pale, boy-opening of his shirt.
All night long, I followed
the fiery climb of his breath
to the metal-cold moon
& back.

Three Sentences

1.

Suppose you are 15 & a virgin
you are behind the barn
suppose he holds your face between his large square fingers
flaked with tobacco & black earth
& his thumb smudges your lip
suppose for a split-second you like it, the warm ripe
granular feel, like running your tongue
over a skinned pear
tiny goose bumps tickle your breasts, suppose
he tells you unzipping his jeans
he needs to get close to you, past your mouth
to someplace his cunt of a wife won't go
suppose the only sound is wheat
shuddering in a spool of wind, your eye catches
the rake falling slow
motion from his hip, you wait
for the thud of the wood pole, but metal teeth
are already glinting from the hay
suppose you want to say God you want to say
mouth torn
you want to say *stop* but now
his farm sweat is behind you shoving
into your body as you struggle
sunlight splintering through the rafters
your voice is somewhere
in the sky whispering from a cloud
thin & faraway.

2.

The week the day the hour the second the
champagne flutes the black garter the Basal thermometer the
Virgin Mary above the bed
the clinically-premeditated sex

he & I & my body
limp fruit, knifed & slit

the three of us lie
drained

I roll the dead thing onto its back
to contain the ocean inside
thighs lined up with the planets
while he disappears
behind a scissor of light to pee.

3.

The small Asian doctor chants the word like a poem
rhyming approximation in broken English—

ster-ile

he falters—
he wants a swab for the petri dish

slow-motion the long metal prod
shatters deep
into the once-blue pond

cauldron of stones
dead fish.

Baby Tech

The tests don't matter, not the icy probe
of his finger, not the flood of purple dye into
the beaten bag of my womb, nothing matters
but the promise of a would-be fetus, fragile
as the wobbling foal
in barn light.

In his lab, bits of women
float in flasks like grains of Aspirin
in a chaos of ginger ale. The one bitter pill
of their lives.

They line up at his door—
their shaman, their priest, God, whatever—
thumbing magazines, eyeing one another, eyeing
his diplomas, like glittering icons on the wall
waiting to see who won, who failed
whose experiment took, whose didn't
they'll all be back next month for more tests
more consultations, they'll lean across his desk
opening their bodies to him
in confession
praying for mercy.

Visit to the Specialist

The eye opens & closes, opens & closes
opens & closes over my file

shiny, phosphorescent bead
swivelling under lizard-lids

his jaded backward gaze
over millennia—

the Big Bang & oceans
unfurled

lush
palm fronds

dinosaurs on the beach floor
clattering in the cold snap.

His look is timed, small hourglass
brain measuring the detail of me.

Outside, a bird rubs against the sky
trying to leave an impression.

One blink
& I am extinguished.

Elemental

Even weeks after the doctor said it, I couldn't look a mug of coffee
in the eye without dredging up all that brown muck
again.

Whoever said spring was pretty, was full of it. Spring is brown.
Snow is yellow or shit-brown, depending. Brown rivers fart
from the bowels of the sewer.

I watch a beetle on my window sill flail upside-down
on its silvery-black shell. The fridge hums its lonely hum.

Brick after grey brick wall. Nobody knows a damn thing.

A bungled chromosome. The hormone pumped into chicken.
Fall-out from a hydro tower. Bad karma.

Me & some awkward boy whose name has slipped away.
Quick snip of hymen & a raspberry blotch widening
on the basement couch while my parents dozed
in white laundered sheets.

A searing hit
of acid.

The night my Inuit lover wrapped me in his parka &
carried me to the nurse, my womb-blood pattering
wine-dark tracks into the snow.

Jeff, whose cold blue eye looked down on me
from his tripod, while I posed open-legged for him
on the blond wood floor of his studio.

Some privy Intelligence, some star
winking from the necklace of Orion.

The Girl at Water's Edge

The world shimmers in its own rain
daffodils in a splash of grass, pregnant women
& their fluid strides, calves gleaming
like quarter-moons.

A secretary waves her diamond ring. Sundays swell
with new moms wheeling prams. Storms of them

& me

like the girl at water's edge
skirt billowing at her knees, envious
of the fish in their naked swim

their undulating trails
of light.

Shadow Play

Sheets hot on my back
I grip the rope of his hair
waiting for the warm, white fizz
to spill us into a champagne world. Again I flounder
eyes drifting to the figures on the wall
skewed shadows fighting for every last stab
of air. An arm, a leg jutting out her back
as though his erect penis were boring
a hole through the keel of her spine
the whole carcass sinking
on a thin raft of light.

Burial

1.

We picnicked in the woods behind the Esso station
on a day brown & drier than a twig, stomachs cool
in the mud, we tickled frogs with a branch
leaned on our elbows, giggling about sex
wondering

how everything fit
together

I didn't stop her
or myself

heat gathering in the folds
of our skin

jigsaw
of cloud overhead

& that restless, pink stone
jailed in the sweat of her palm.

2.

The thing about trying to make a baby
is that you tend to focus on the abstraction
& ignore the moment

the dying mandarin sun, bananas freckling in a bowl
strands of his freshly-shampooed hair falling
across your cheek.

Specialists & test tubes & thermometers
have dulled all senses

left my anatomy splayed in a V
no sparkling June watermelon
bleeding in a dish, no blue-red embryo

no Victory

only a small parched mouth
between my thighs

& the senselessness of it all.

3.

Some memories
you bury—

the bare humidity
on your apricot vagina.

You pretend you were on a picnic
or that you never masturbated as a kid
but the past is still there, lurking

nerve ends fingered to ecstasy
the forbidden touch, stolen
glances at one another

the distortion of our faces & mouths
as the pink stone disappeared inside, cool marble
on the ball of our sex

panties buried by a tree-trunk
in the bluish mud.

Family Tree

Years from now, I'll be a stranger
in the family tree, footnote yellowing
in the back pages of an album
along with the rest—

wives pencilled in, girls who crossed fences
into white-steepled towns
diluting the blood, guests
to the ancestral home
mismatched linens & china patterns
clashing with the furniture

stick-figure children who died of consumption
ropy phlegm killing off entire branches
of the tree, long lines of men
who might have sprouted at their hand
shadowy profiles planting the soil
in the shape of their memories.

Poem for the Dead

My husband weeps under a bare light bulb
brooding in the worm-glow
of his parents, two pale slugs in the ground

dreams the walls of their hearts, the reassuring steam
of blood, their warm human sounds.

He reaches for the old house
gentle tug of their faces
like porch lanterns on a January night.

Yesterday, when the furnace went
we boarded up windows
trying to stave off the cold bone-structure
of winter.

In my dream, a kid shivered by the stove
the collapsed house around him.

Late Afternoon

Winter's thrown me off kilter
the way new neighbours
change the feel of a place, their havoc
of mittens & scarves along a porch railing
chipped toys junking the yard, one flashy red toboggan
& an entire street lit with new meaning.

A house like that moves in its own time.

I gaze at their Christmas world, winking
red & green lights, the intricate link
of mother & son on opposite arms of a sofa
lifting a bright paper chain to the window.

He, leaving oily thumbprints
she, clapping at the stove
boiling cocoa & marshmallows.

The sun visits me briefly now

a pale nod of light
across the snow.

Two Women

for Margaret Webb

Maggie left her husband & job to agonize
over poetry in Montreal

peopling her apartment
with books & theory

says it is enough
just being

on a lawn chair
with a litre of red wine & her journal
boundless
blue sky clapping above.

2.

You wonder if life
means something messier
than a bungalow in the suburbs

something more in line
with bug spray & scaly turquoise paint.

You drift blank-eyed into space
picturing how good it would feel to walk barefoot
across her pine-planked floors
clay mug of coffee in hand, books in hectic piles
on the bed

alone & dizzy with poetry
long black T-shirt
hanging free.

3.

3 o'clock & neither of us has gotten up once to pee
smoking at a lopsided card table by the balcony
nothing moving outside but the wavy August heat
above the curb.

She opens another bottle & we drink
some more, glass after glass of warm red wine.

She's radiant about some lesbian
theory she discovered in a book, a dream
she had last night & she's hammering out a new poem

talks with her hands, her whole body
flying, those weird echoes
next door like the blood rushing
in her veins or her fingers pounding the keyboard.

Meanwhile I'm thinking it's years since I've had a dream
I can remember & I'm half-listening, half-falling

down a thin glass tube
of ether, into sweet-jesus blue
nothing.

The Underworld

On the count of ten, you, spread-eagle on the table. Technician
swabbing an iodine-brown sun onto your belly. At eight
the room grey, pebbly. A voice, finally catching the ear. Breaking
as it hits. The whitest wafer of light closing in on itself to black.
The hiss as it goes, an earthquake rocking the body. Last quiver
up the spine.

Stuff of the room going watery. You, slipping. Arms & legs scissored
apart, falling deeper & deeper into the dark vault. Grooves of the body
ballooning & distorting with water. Blue bits of sky blinking light-years
above the hemispheres of the brain. Body emptying itself of itself
dissolving into the clammy black air. Bare threads of you drifting
like old pink Kleenex at the bottom of a sewer.

Part of you here, part of you there.

The long black rat when I was ten & playing behind a factory.
Fur gummed back & glinting in the sun. The garbage lid I whacked it
with until the bones were good & crushed. As if that wasn't enough.
The small grey mice I hid downstairs in the laundry room for a school
project. Starving & poking them until their rabid snouts
finally turned on one another.

Driving Home from the Hospital

I breathe & he breathes, he asks if I'm chilled
fiddles with the dash, the radio
jogs the vents, I am exhausted watching him.
A frail snowflake trembles at the windshield
dissolves under the eyelash
of a long black wiper.

Just when I thought I could count on him, he arrived
with my release papers & a long-stemmed rose
tender folds like the inner regions
of a woman. How he had the audacity—
this reminder of loss, this small death.

On peut toujours adopter, he says
turning up the driveway, words awakening in him
like a final burst of summer. I can't share his energy, his enthusiasm
drawn, instead, to the grey-brown scraggle in our garden
the pocked terrain, recalling the cosmos
before they withered into nothing.
Tall, hardy, dancing
in the wind.

Parallel Thoughts:
Driving Home from the Hospital

Ali McGraw & Ryan O'Neal
in their famous poster-clutch.
The vinyl beanbag chair & pink record player.
Crackly 45's, those old summer hits. *Spinning Wheel.*
Spines of forbidden books turned inward on the shelf.
Love Story. Summer of 42.

My own secret novels
tucked in a drawer under rolls of socks.
A tentative *fuck* or two for splash. Written in code
in case Mum ever found them. Parts of the word
left blank.

That collision of F & K, the sour wince in your throat
rising like vomit, the beefy groan. Dry shock of
the penis. Your father's
stash of *Playboy* magazines. What men did
to women. That word.

Just thinking all this, warm lips
of rain passing the window.

Your closed bedroom door, the slow creep of hair
at your neck. Legs midair, panties a thin ring at your ankles
dropping the pen first & then the book
fingers working the whole
unbroken yolk, that small cry from within, the fear
of entry, of things you are & are not
capable of.

Ambivalence. That song.

Enough to last a lifetime.

Under This Moon

I know by the bloat of the moon I've got my period again.
The way the warm wind carries my blood
back to me, as the clay-red earth sends
its own menstrual odor back in spring.

Under this moon, under this black, dimensionless sky
where you want connections between this & that—
solid reasons for things.

The dull, brown river pulling through me
eggs in a downward spin
like the yolk of dead corpses
on the six o'clock news.

Under this moon, where one sideways glance
opens our bodies to every new sore on the planet—

the pain, for instance, of the child across the street
knees hugged into her chest
tears of the moon falling into the small cup
of her body.

Shaking your fist, you're actually thinking—God
damn it, give me one, just one good reason
why I can't have a baby & you're literally screaming
bloody murder

which is why you find yourself desperate
for a connection
between the girl in the thin cotton dress & the ivy
worming up the trellis like a cancer, nailing its shadow
to the crumbling mortar of the house.
Or the girl & her father
caught in a slur of kitchen light
stumbling back & forth into an avocado
green stove, core of his body
pitted with darkness.

A simple connection—

like the one between the rasping
wind & the stir of new blossoms
mouthing for air.

Prognosis

1.

We drive
from the surgeon's office, spotless
cubicle where my spidery X-ray flickered
on a thin white screen, where he delivered
the bite, cool & clipped
as a weather report—

Your chances are less than 5%

Driving, neither of us speaks
slow pupils drifting like dull black zeroes.
The tarry summer heat swims off the road.
Every angle of concrete hisses
under the sun, blanched.

At the Wellington Tunnel, traffic stalls
& cars creep in the humid dark
like the lesions in my fallopian tubes
the doctor sliced away.

2.

Nothing registers but every wrong rub against me
the fibrous weave of the car seat
crawling up the backs of my thighs
every knife & intrusive hack at my body
my husband's hand bumping mine
hot & real as the ash on a burning cigarette
one pulls away from
that shooting nerve
of pain.

Intuition tells me
the lumps & scars will root again
raggy tentacles spreading in profusion, baby heads
of cabbage, tender & green, multiplying
in the warm trench of my womb.

Eyes averted, we listen to the radio
& wait.

Scars

An old love affair
lingers, untamed

catches my skin every autumn
like the jagged edges of a leaf

the raw pulsating thing
where my heart should be, meat
of it lifting to the music of the moon.

How we glittered in our animal pockets
of water, doing it to Mahler & Stan Getz & every one of the
Brandenburg Concertos.

Another year gone
& that feline madness again

jazz on a street corner
a small rooming house on Marie-Anne

the roar
of a yellow leaf.

Nightmare

Partying at Jennifer's—cigarettes & wine & suddenly a telephone
balloons in my hand, treble voice shrieking about a friend
getting hit by the Metro

a million thoughts rush thru my mind, his house, his car, his bank
account, his girlfriend, his live voice on the answering machine

can you take the Metro home right away? she asks, the voice an old
family neighbour whose husband once pestered me all the way
to my dorm room, phone ringing & ringing off the hook until
I unplugged it, the creepy lecherous *brrring* of it, zapped him
into thin air with all the other insects, later his rotten seed converged
in the baby they made, a sick kid with a sick little mind

can you take the Metro home? cn you tke the Metro home?
Tk th Metro hm   Metro Metro   Metro
she obviously wants me dead, this woman

psychoanalyzing the crazy mixed-up pieces, replaying it
scene by scene, the message, the voice, peeling it back to the bare nerve
waiting for a severed black hand to reach around
the bathroom door when I least expect it

Can YOU take the Metro
& then dead air.

Limbo

It's taking forever to peel an orange
fingers jammed in time
though, far as I know
I'm not dead yet.

Reds & plaids are bleeding over me
I want 'em all, flying specks of anything
every decimal of colour
& negative space.

Conversation's on a hellward bend
multiplying exponentially
like the white, painted lines on a highway
never-ending.

We're hanging by the bare thread
of a window, & this fucking orange
is way too big
for any of us.

Mister Falafel

I smoke by the January window
reflection & I

dark rinse of traffic
outside

leaning umbra
of a coffee mug

grey mushroom
wall

ashtray, a crumpled foil heart
on the table.

I smoke the cigarette, filling a small chair
with myself.

Two

The Palmist

for Rhonda

The moon chases the dark
for its other half.

My hands in clammy leather, the black highway
splash of cars as I wait for a bus, wait for her

to trace the fault lines
in my palm

blue TV light in a corner
of the room, soft noise

of her touch realigning the planets
birthing a child.

A fine dream of snow passes the window
& we are laughing now

huddled by the stove, fingers warming
thin china cups.

Waiting for the bus home, the top-heavy sky
lifts away. Even the crazy metal of cars
holds new meaning.

Foreshadowing

When I finally let go
of science, I remembered the story of Moses
how his own mother defied the Pharaoh
& wove her baby into a nest of bulrushes

how she let him go
as one lets go of consciousness in sleep
she, alone at the riverbed, a pinpoint
against the darkening sky
cool dry breeze emptying
the heat from her body

& I thought of the Pharaoh's daughter who found him
curled on his side like a small animal
limbs tucked under his body
twitching lightly

nameless, motherless
drifting into the wide-open
hands of God.

Khamseen*

The plane lands
like a small typhoon.

Passengers jostle on the tarmac
throats dry as cumin.

We board the mushroom darkness of a bus
raw wind bending around us

where nothing moves
but the odd molecule & Assaad's face
lifting from a dry scrap of paper.

The Syrian President
eyes us from every parched wall
of Customs. He is in every russet uniform
every cocked rifle, every broom-thick moustache

every red coal of every cigarette.

His earth-cracked lips heave & harden
under the volcano of words.

Somewhere in the desert
the small spine of a cactus
shivers.

---

* An extremely dry, stifling, sand-laden wind which originates in the North African Sahara, and lasts for approximately 50 days.

The Fertile Crescent

Bedouin women
in a cobbler's doorway
cross-legged with their baskets
of eggs & vine leaves

eyewhites, a dull glaze

babies in their laps
like steaming loaves of bread.

Death is a distant country to them
a great, green curve of land
where ancestors wait
unburdened—

mosaic of upturned faces
like golden plates of fruit
in the sun.

Man in a Doorway I

At first glance it is nothing more than a ghost town
of mortar & withered car parts
a nothing blink of the eye
but somewhere under the dead winter sky
below the stump of a broken building
a human hand appears
like the first stir of grass.

A small man under a burrow
of light sells figs & fava beans
from a bright red cart. He is whistling.

Beirut has begun to thaw.

Second Look

photograph of Lebanon, 1982

Skeletal ruins on the fringe
of town. Cracked walls & live wires
shivering in the wind. The greys of the shack
are muted, shades of devastation
too subtle for the lens

an image easily forgotten, unremarkable
as the peasant headed for the rubble
long black veils vanishing in the air. Her hand
clutches a transparent white bag through which
we make out the bare bones
of groceries, figs & a shoulder of lamb

but follow her gaze past fragments
of twisted junipers & cypress trees, her boy
tagging barefoot behind

that fierceness in her eye
like the last grove of cedars
surviving in the mountains.

The Survivors

The Lebanese endure their lives
even in death
Syrians stomping all over them
barking commands.

Once a deaf man got it
from behind, cornered animal
like a decimal on the leaden horizon

pressure building inside the hollow drum of his ear
long, lean haunches gobbling up
the forward-moving pavement
until the explosion came

small click in his ear
like the last sputter of radio, silvery sound
waves thinning into the primordial base
of his brain.

Neighbours dragged the dead weight of his body
up a steep flight & into a limestone house
head bobbing sideways from its stem.

No one acknowledged the wound
until they laid out the huge bulk of him
& noticed a halo of blood
soaking into the Persian knots of the rug.

No one saw death come
floating into his mouth, only the big dark ant
that crawled along his blank eye
& onto his faltering tongue

the last speck of life
he took in.

Man in a Doorway II

Old tawny fingers scattering the worry
along his rosary, beads blunt & smooth as bullets

who never cried when they shelled his house
not even when he lifted his son's head
by its twisted nape & carried him out of the fire.

He rests under the tired hood
of his eye. This is God's will
it seems to say.

I pity him. Shorn white head, the way his reverent
toes curl under the frayed hemp of his sandals.

Around him the street is levelled. Chances are
he won't live to see the new world rise up
from the rubble, brassy cafés
with bold awnings & gilt-edged tables
where men in fine suits will smoke & haggle
over cobalt-blue thimbles of Arabic coffee
afternoon clouds rearranging the sky.

I memorize the scene
like some mantra.

This making & unmaking of the world.

Origins

1.

In another version
a paranoid Joseph
exiles Mary to the desert
to escape her tyrant father
who might slaughter them both.

She wanders among the Bedouins
veiled & anonymous
across the shifting dunes.

On a clear night
the camels form a mystic circle around her
while she coughs the bloodwet child
through a slit in her body

names him Fady
like Jesus in Hebrew
bundles him in goat-hair & leaves him
on a barren woman's doorstep
limp & wrinkled, perfect animal
of her womb

begs a star in the East
to light her way back.

2.

My cousin gives birth during a cease-fire
weaves the infant in eggshell blue
& chances the mountain
sky bright as brass.

Suddenly
war splits the air

shell burst
& random shapes
catching the windshield

dust & wind in all directions
like confetti. She gropes among pieces
of the car floor, sheltering the boy
in the large tent of her body

& fanfare
scatters the knoll.

La Place des Martyrs

(1991)

They gather here
as though a party were about to break, anarchy
of card tables & broken lawn chairs
soda pop & cigarettes.

Or perhaps the party is over & the rubble
is really the aftermath of a good time, champagne toss
of peanut shells & confetti on New Year's Eve.

A man licks an ice-cream cone
another shuffles randomly, wondering what to sweep
leftover kids straddle the chipped wings of a statue.

16 years of war
200,000 dead.

Everyone moves cautiously in his skin
waiting for the hangover to set in.

House in the Bekaa

Travelogue shock
of white & Aegean blue.

Empty sky & one house
bleached as a Greek villa—

though this is no
holiday town.

Shell-pocked walls

rungs connecting the ramshackle frame of a ladder
ladder connecting the lizard ground
to a flat mud roof

where children might sit throwing stones
legs swung over the edge
or a sunburnt pilgrim might pause
for a brown jug of water
on his difficult journey
to heaven.

Crèche Saint-Vincent-de-Paul

for Soeur Bassoul & Soeur Madeleine

1.

The nun wipes her forehead
with the knobby back of her hand
leads us beyond the garden wall
where lemons the size of grapefruits
hang thick in their skins
against a mirror of blue

childhood summers surfacing
in each spike of light.

Dandelions lifting their yellow skirts
in the breeze. Warm waft of *citronelle*
as I peddle Dixie cups from a red wagon
bumping along the sidewalk
with my clinking tin of nickels

money for a new doll
to lay in the shining grass.

2.

For a moment, there is nothing
in the air but a dumb gaze
like that instant after a relative dies
as one kneels in the half-light
by the ashen corpse, breathless

then a faint stir as the soul lifts
& crosses out of the darkness.

I wait on the cool green marble
sun angling down from a tall window
moment filled with coughs & echoes of coughs
& the long bar of light streaming in & then
a nun in her blue habit
materializes at the door.

In that first breath we take together
I have already memorized
every detail of you, every nuance, the fine weave
of your hair, each nutmeg-brown stitch
the pale pink braid of your skin.

Deep inside my body
the first pulse of you.

Heading for the Canadian Embassy in Damascus

Pawns on a board
we wait for his hand to move us
into safe terrain, George Asslan
the poker-faced driver with a smile
crooked as the dealers at the Souk
their golden teeth glinting
like bullets.

He does it for the money
sneaks people in & out of Syria
long, dark sedan smoking Beirut at 4 A.M.
greeting the Bekaa
at the first clang of day.

He knows the game
gaze like a snake's-eye toss of the dice
barters with large, flat coins of bread & Marlboro cigarettes.

Nothing fazes him—not the bulging eyes of the guard
like pure black weapons
not the scarf-headed Moslem women whispering
on their swayback mules
in the caged light
of dawn.

rue Hamra

Slit-eyed in shadeless West Beirut
combing maps for a sign
a landmark, any point of reference
the day, a haze
of dust & coriander.

The driver circles & circles for parking
wiping oil from his forehead, drops
us somewhere to pick through
olive-grey boards & fallen plaster
baby gathered into my breasts, into the very nucleus
of my being, the pressure of his weight
entering me, every rosy particle of matter
the sunny planet of his face.

Soon the world begins
to fall away from us, spinning on its own congested axis
as though we no longer need it
the noise, the traffic, the silvery-white light
as though we can finally be everything
to each other

the sun, the moon, the stars.

Three

The Meeting Place

Nights I dream a rambling vineyard
with pendulous purple grapes &
the Arabian horse my grandmother rode
to single-handedly drive the Turks
from her father's land. I see her youthful hair
catching the wind, the old stone house in Zahlé
where she lived with seven sisters, the family womb
& its vast spiral of blood. I see fish spawning
in the river, the rippling effect. I see my boy
like a dormant seed in her path
waiting for its moment of sun.

Birth Poem

1.

Kitchen window.
Egglight.

Raisins in their swollen
bowl of milk.

Nipples dark, enlarged.
Wet, wide-open cunt.

An infant, thrusting its head
like a new seed

splitting
the light.

2.

The nun releases
her long, silken braid

strokes my breast
bringing a flood of milk.

Jesus smiles
from the cross.

We come together
on the small cot, trembling.

3.

Land of bloodied buildings
& hollow grass. The moon
an open gash in the sky.

Birth-mother drifts
along the beach
hugging the wounded stem
of her body

thin, stockinged feet
roaming the shoreline
contour of a ribcage
poking through her pale dress

random prints in the sand
starting nowhere, ending
nowhere.

The Little Things

Infant in my arms
blissful angel in the dust of sleep
fingers laced with mine
white gauze curtains
gentling over us.

A breeze from the open window
ruffles his hair, honeyed
in the moonlight.

We fill the room like lovers
in our rumpled bed

languid & content.

Root

How I saved your umbilical cord
in a Birks box, wrapped in tissue
with your first shoes & a lock of hair

how when my mother bathed you it fell away
& she delivered it on a bed of Kleenex
part of the tree from which you hung like amber fruit
in another woman's womb

how my mother's shining eyes met mine

how she handed it to me the way a neighbour
shares a clipping from her garden
hoping it will take root.

Woman Whose Baby Died of S.I.D.S.

I wonder how often she replays it in her mind—
the clumsy warnings of the day, pressure cooker screaming
in the kitchen, fitful shift of sky.

The new mother, sensing an odd configuration
bolts from a deep grunt of sleep & fumbles
to the crib, racing the lime-green stitch of digits
around the clock-radio, only her feet are already
carrying her backwards by then

as though Earth were suddenly running
out of time & stars were unravelling
like spools of thread, slipping
through the dark, empty knot of space
random bits of her life recurring
in a dull loop, cheating on a physics test
the guy she stole from her best friend
crazed interface of the universe
weaving in & out of her path

to the hush
of that baby's room.

Mothers

They said the woman who stuffed her newborn into a bus-station locker
sealed him like a piece of meat inside a freezer bag.
Nobody got why someone with a clipped lawn
& perfect life could do such a thing.

Picture the cloistered nun
who, as a child, mothered all her siblings
& then whimsically flung the maternal bones from the shrine
of her body.

Or the girl in the abortion clinic
barely a woman yet
having the gelatin yanked from her womb.
She's heard too much of the bad stuff, the factory lives
whole neighbourhoods bred & rebred with each other
until everyone comes out looking the same—

large, domed foreheads
freakish bodies
wide, hammock grins.

She wouldn't be caught dead.

Picture the frazzled one in the grocery line
placating her cranky kid with Sweet Tarts & chips
secretly praying the next one is dead when it's pulled
white as an uncooked goose from the stove of her belly.

A woman leaves sanity behind
the way she leaves an old umbrella on the bus
excess baggage weighing her down

steps off the bright rod of light into a dark neighbourhood
a smudge of time around midnight
when Monday becomes Tuesday
because of a mere cosmic shift, a momentary blur
when all she can see are gardens & their off-centre flowers
& the moon swinging upside-down from the trees.

The Way It Is

When you ask me
who built the sky
I'll say this—

Some engineer with a
designer mug, car phone
& blueprint his boss drafted
with a gold pen
on a plane ride to Cayman.

All I know is
order sneaks up on us
conformity
what you can & cannot get away with.

We spend our afternoons together
on the Oriental rug
me piling pink blocks
one by one, patterns
of letters & numbers
for your balled fist to swat

grey winter days stacked
against you.

Balancing

for my grandmother

My boy, perched on a knee
when the phone call comes. Shrill, final, one ring.
He convulses in my arms, pink pelting screams
for a feeding or diaper change. They say the stroke reduced her
to a coma, then death. I tend to my son
spooning formula into water, gentling his mouth
over the small, porous nipple.

Sickness was her life. This doctor & that.
Mornings, from bed to the overheated den
with her loud television & fifty pill bottles
rattling on the couch. Waist shrinking
until her robe hung loose as bunting
over the brittle porcelain
of her bones.

After the funeral, I prop Alex on an apple branch
observing the boy at my hand, the contradictions
every hearty cell of his body, his fragility
like the pale lilac on the verge of a moment
ready to enter this world completely
ready to leave it anytime.

Baptism

We gather in Byzantine light
chant of rain through tall, stained windows.
The priest circles a brass font of water
baby raised in his arms like a chalice.
He is dipped & delivered to me
in wool & soft boughs
of cedar, cleansed
protected.

On the street, amber headlights
illuminate the pagan wind, the broken lives
in our path—

boozer in a doorway speaking in tongues
bag-lady carting her muddled possessions
through the spattering rain.

They stumble in the dark
jittering bodies misinterpreting space
as though somewhere along the line
they missed a step.

The air rushes its cool prayer through me
as I bundle Alex for the walk home
holy oil gleaming from his forehead
like a burnished weapon
against the world.

Alex at 2

He uses his lips like weapons
attacking the air, firing nouns & verbs
like heavy artillery.

The superfluous stuff—articles & prepositions
—lay low in the trench of his mouth
a muddle of sound.

He wields a stick, the biggest & longest
drags it clicking along the sidewalk
leaving mud trails behind
his own small mark
on the world.

At the sandbox, he stakes his claim
one tough little jean jacket shrugging off the sun
a surrender of girls by the swings.

Me! he shouts, *Me!*
bold as a brass jet
of toddler pee.

Connecting

He is learning my language, I am learning
his. I read *Hop on Pop*. Simple words, easy
for a kid.

He vomits after dinner, gags
on milk & mashed potatoes.

I mop the spoiled
hieroglyphs.

He is upset, jumpy, unable to sit
for a quiet moment, body wired to its own
grammar of space & time.

He darts around the den, runs
for a power cord, then another, makes a beeline for the stereo
testing every button, every switch. At bath time he devises a
popcorn machine, a furnace out of old yoghurt containers & plastic lids
wonders how fast he can dump the Lego blocks
how much racket
he can make.

Finally, his rhythm slows. He curls up
beside me like a comma.

Mami.

For a breath
we connect.

Alex's Leaf

The leaf he finds is ugly, bleached white
like a hand starred with detergent, burnt at the tips
its mottled underside the brown of liver spots or
old tea stains.

I twirl it, wondering what he loves about this dead
thing, wondering why he didn't choose the one beside it
scarlet & teeming with energy

its own spun planet of rain & mown grass.

Instead, he picked the corpse in its airtight grave
every stiff cell clenched with sleep

embracing it, unconditionally
for what it is.

Coastal Maine (Higgins Beach)

1.

In twenty years it hasn't changed
same smells, same
hump in the beach road
before that first blue jag of water &
the sun jumping like sequins off the sand

the cool, fishy breeze that runs
goose bumps down our arms at sunset
as we stand at the lip of the marsh
watching Alex in soggy runners
seaweed looped in olive bracelets
around his small, centipede fingers.

2.

As a kid I never trusted
the beach—

surf in random time
each speck of sand
an erosion.

My mother combed the finny slate
to keep us in arts & crafts all winter
shells & salmon stones to paint
bunched heather & blackened twists of driftwood
for Christmas decorations. She saw possibilities
in everything—

damp, springy sand
the potent healing salt
of the ocean

a cottage's splintered
beauty.

Taking the Fall

Alex has begun to build. He fingers
the Lego blocks, dazzled by their
solid, plastic strength. Unaware
of pattern & form, unaware of probability, he piles them
in pure random order, a naive masterpiece.

The tower is dangerously lopsided.

There's a lever for the furnace, a chimney
for the smoke to come out. His trusting eyes gleam, his
cheeks puff like dough on a cookie sheet, as he lets go
& claps for his monstrosity. In that split second
I catch it all—
the bad report card, the girl who leaves him
by an open door, vanishing point
in a bleak, oblong of space

the plummeting structure I can't catch
fast enough.

Her

I can tell by your face that
she is beautiful
full red lips, spirited laugh
someone you will search all your life for
with the same energy
you dig the earth in our garden
lashes starred with mud

peering into your dark empty hole
the way you hunt for the perfect twig
or the missing piece
of a puzzle

curious back of your head trailing
unknown streets & unknown people
the absent one
as she slowly takes shape
in your eye.

This Poem

How can I let this poem
get in the way of my kissing him good night
mere words—after all—nothing as earth-shattering
as his story about the yellow digger at the construction site
industrious steel arm hauling mounds of dirt & concrete
through the sky. Somewhere on the edge of my pen
his thin voice is rising & falling
getting in the way
of words

nothing on the page but a vague impression
of him huddled with Pooh Bear
in his flannel bed, yawning in the dark
& his pale, pink lids surrendering to the moths
in the apple light of a place
far, far away.

About the Author

Carolyn Marie Souaid was raised and educated in Montreal, Quebec. She holds an MA from Concordia University and a teaching degree from McGill. Over the years, she has worked as an educator, freelance journalist, and magazine columnist.

Her poetry has appeared in a wide variety of literary publications including *Quarry, PRISM International,* and *The Urban Wanderers Reader* (Hochelaga Press).

For several years, Souaid taught elementary school in Inuit villages along the Hudson and Ungava coasts of Arctic Quebec. She has also taught at Concordia University and currently teaches high school English to Adult Education students in a Montreal suburb.

In 1992, Souaid and her husband travelled to Lebanon to adopt their infant son. It was her first trip to her ancestral homeland.

Achevé d'imprimer en octobre 1995 chez

à Boucherville, Québec